H. P. Blanchard

A visit to Japan in 1860 in the U.S. frigate "Hartford"

H. P. Blanchard

A visit to Japan in 1860 in the U.S. frigate "Hartford"

ISBN/EAN: 9783743442023

Manufactured in Europe, USA, Canada, Australia, Japa

Cover: Foto ©ninafisch / pixelio.de

Manufactured and distributed by brebook publishing software
(www.brebook.com)

H. P. Blanchard

A visit to Japan in 1860 in the U.S. frigate "Hartford"

A VISIT TO JAPAN

IN 1860

IN THE

U. S. FRIGATE "HARTFORD"

AND

A RETURN FROM CHINA BY THE U. S. S. FRIGATE "NIAGARA"
TO ADEN AND THENCE *VIA* THE RED SEA AND EUROPE
TO THE UNITED STATES.

H. P. B.

SAN FRANCISCO:

1878.

October 8th, 1860, Monday.

My very dear Mother :

I addressed a letter to you from Shanghai by the last mail, in which I advised my intended departure for Nagasaki and Kanagawa, in this ship, a guest of the ward-room officers, and I might add, of the captain, for it is in his cabin where my own state-room is assigned me. I passed ten days at Shanghai in visiting and being received by friends there con. nected with various commercial houses, and left with regret, for I like the people and the place. Whenever the Chinese Empire settles into order, its government becomes firm and universal, and trade assumes its once universal importance and regularity throughout the length and breadth of the land, the rivers become open to our steamers, and the rebellion subsides, Shanghai, by its position, will become the most important port. It sits upon the Woosung river, near the Yang-tze-Kiang, which will float down upon its bosom, ere many years, and in our own steamers too, the increasing products of the most productive provinces of the Central and Flowery Kingdom. The mail which went last, conveyed to you the failure of the attempt at double dealing on the part of the Chinese commissioner with Lord Elgin at Tientsin, and the advance to within five miles of Pekin, of the English and French forces, where, and where alone, Lord Elgin says he will now negotiate. But now I will turn to myself.

I came on board this ship on Friday noon. We started at 2.P.M., and steamed down river, passing Woosung at 3 P.M., and at 10 P.M. we discharged our pilot, and were at sea. During our trip down river, the United States steam dispatch boat, " Saginaw," passed us with Mr. Ward on board. He left an hour after us, bound to Hong-Kong. Saturday, our first day at sea, was calm and delightful, our ship steaming eight knots per hour, no canvas set, through a smooth sea. I will just add here, that Nagasaki is four hundred and twenty miles from Shanghai, and that to-day, at noon, we were still one hundred and forty miles distant. On Sunday, our second day, our calm was interrupted. The pure, cold northeast wind poured down through the straits of Corea the strength of the monsoon, and with a high sea, impeded our progress, as it was in our teeth, exactly. But though the day was so rough as to prevent having divine service, yet it was nothing to the succeeding night. I think even you, with all your forbearance and patience, would have been positively miserable. The fresh breezes of the day increased at night to a moderate gale, while the sea rolled against our sides, causing the huge ship to tremble and shake from stem to stern. I slept upon my stateroom floor, for to keep in my berth was too much of an experiment to trust to. I made the passage from New York to China without once being seasick; but I confess, last night brought me to a compromise. I was very seasick for half an hour. To-day, Monday, has been quiet, and the ship moving gently, though the northeast wind is too strong to allow us to keep on our course. And now I will speak of the ship.

She is a fine model for sailing; and is intended for sailing, not for steaming, though the propeller is a good one, yet only intended for calms and to act as an auxiliary. She is of about eighteen hundred tons register, about 230 feet long. She has on board 336, crew and officers, beside Mr. Coolidge of Boston, a young Mr. Fearing (a guest of the midshipmen) and myself. Commodore, or rather flag-officer Stribling, has his cabin by himself, below on the same deck with the wardroom officers. Captain Loundes, an elderly gentleman, has his cabin on the upper deck; while the wardroom below contains five lieutenants, three surgeons, purser, master, commodore's clerk (Charles Downes) and captain and sergeant of marines. These are all very kind to me, and do all they can to make me a welcome and satisfied guest. The table is excellent, and though all are extremely temperate, yet constant jollity and pleasantry enlivens every meal. By the way, the engineer-in-chief is a wardroom officer. The crew is divided, as is usual in a man-of-war, into bodies styled fore, main and mizzen topmen, into watches of ninety men each, and then all are under the orders, respectively, of the officer of the deck or lieutenant, relieved every four hours, boatswain and captain of the tops. A body of thirty marines are also a part of the company. They dress on week days, in light blue trowser and jacket, with a glazed cap on the front of which is " U. S. M." On Sundays, at ten, they appear at quarters in full uniform — a flowing feather in high hats and a handsome uniform. This term, "going to quarters," I will explain. But first, let me give you the daily routine of the ship. At 8 A.M. the flag is hoisted, while the band, consisting

of twelve pieces, play the "Star Spangled Banner."
We then breakfast at ten A.M.; the drum rolls and
every one goes to quarters, that is, appear on deck,
the officers with side arms, and the men are ranged
along in their respective bodies ; each lieutenant has
his, the engineer all his, except those attending the
engine; the captain of marines has his men drawn
up in a double line, muskets in hand ; every gun of
the battery has its quota of men at its station, twelve
at each ; the lieutenants, the captain of marines and
the chief engineer then step forward and salute the
commander, announcing his respective division to be
in order and present, which he, in turn, acknowledges
by touching his hat. All this time, perfect silence is
maintained, and immediately the commander has received the report of the officers, and during this silence,
the chaplain steps forward and makes a prayer, every
head, of course, uncovered. This over, the men dis-
perse ; the officers send their side arms below, and
nothing more ensues than the ordinary duties of sailing the ship, until 4 P.M., when the same is gone
through with. The band then comes aft and plays an
hour, and this finishes the day. Target practice at
sea, is very common, but we have had none as yet; the
weather being bad has kept us back, and now we have
no time to stop the ship for it.

The "Hartford" can carry a battery of twenty-six
eight-inch shell guns, but she has now sixteen nine-
inch shell guns, weighing from nine to ten thousand
pounds each—a beautiful battery, and all on the upper
or main deck.

I am writing you while we are moving on toward the
coast of Japan, at the slow rate of seven miles per

hour, with contrary wind. She rolls considerably, and therefore 'tis not easy to write; but I am beginning this early, as if we get into Nagasaki, I shall wish to have a line ready for you. So far as I know now, it is intended that this ship shall remain at Nagasaki four days, then proceed in charge of two government pilots through what is termed the "inland sea," remarkable for the wonders of its scenery, to Kanagawa, some five hundred miles, the seaport of, and distant from Jeddo eighteen miles. This remarkable inland sea is said to take us along the main land and through innumerable island passages, where cultivation on all sides, with high lands, render the whole passage the most beautiful conceivable. Charles Downes, the commodore's secretary, told me he had told him he should anchor every night, and run day times, in order to see the beauties of this passage. This is one of the advantages I possess in being in this ship. It is expected that the "Niagara" will soon reach Kanagawa with the Japanese commissioners, and very probably a party will then be invited to go to Jeddo. If so, I trust I may be one. You may not, however, be aware that though the respective ministers reside at Jeddo, yet no citizens of any country are allowed to go up, except by invitation of the minister. Report says, that our minister lives at Jeddo, in a state of inebriety and immorality, which, with the advantage of seclusion from his countrymen, affords him additional ground for refusing to invite or see them.

I might have said that on the first afternoon of our being at sea, just at sundown, the shrill whistle of the mate, followed by the hoarse roar of the boatswain's, "All hands attend to bury the dead," resounded fore and aft. Every one was present whose duty could be set aside, service read, and the body slid into the blue sea, which closed over it.

Mr. Coolidge I find a delightful man, and have had many an hour pacing the deck or sitting in conversation with him. He says he belongs to a Wednesday club with Dr. Homans, but as he is away so much, I should think he could seldom be present at it. He left home last May.

I hope the "Judge Shaw" arrived all right, with those toilet sets, unbroken; if not, I shall be *furious*. Ain't you afraid? Well, I must stop. I have been writing in the first lieutenant's room. I will go up now, have a chat with the commander and turn in, as we say. I hope not only you and all our family, but also that uncle George is well.

October 10th. I wrote the last two leaves at sea, this one I commence in the harbor of Nagasaki, at but 9 P.M., after having been at anchor a day and a night. We arrived here last evening, at 7 P.M., (the 9th). The harbor entrance is narrow and beautiful, the land high on either hand, and cultivated from the edge of the sea to a thousand feet up the highlands. Every hill, every foot of soil, everywhere is cultivated in beds or patches, except at the tops of the mountains, where woods are permitted to grow. As we entered the harbor, we passed the cliffs, where, in 1500, many thousands of christians perished in being hurled down by order of the government; that was when 800,000 christians were destroyed in Japan. This, too, is the city where the poor Macao catholics in 1520, were beheaded ; a scene represented by the old painting now in Macao, of which I have written you before. As we first made the land we discovered the fact of great depth of water, bold shores and volcanic character of the hills; in fact, we saw a hill upon an island, emitting smoke, where, 'tis said, some fourteen volcanoes exist. You can, perhaps, understand the feeling that came over me, when last evening our anchor dropped from this beautiful ship into this beautiful harbor. The idea that I was in Japan, in a port known to the Dutch for two centuries, I could not realize. Of course, 'twas too late last evening to go on shore, so we waited until this A.M. at 10. The captain of a Russian man-of-war called last evening, also a Dutch lieutenant and a messenger from the English consul.

This morning, at quarter before nine, the Dutch saluted us, and at nine the Russians; both salutes we immediately returned—twenty-six guns. At 10 A.M., Mr. Coolidge, myself and six wardroom officers took the third cutter and were pulled ashore by a man-of-war's crew of twelve men. Here we received our first impressions of Japan and the Japanese. We visited Nagasaki, as also the Dutch settlement known as Decima. This Decima is the island which the Dutch, for two centuries, have been allowed to land upon, when their one vessel a year came from Holland to Japan; and I have to-day walked over that identical stone bridge, which connects the island with Nagasaki, and which you may recollect old Mr. Gregerson once said at our house he had crossed, when a boy at sea—as a cabin boy in a Dutch ship—in the capacity of servant to the captain. 'Tis a short bridge, only fifty feet wide and as long, but 'tis remarkable when you contrast the restraint once laid upon foreigners in crossing it, who five years ago would have met death in attempting it, and to-day we have been all over the town. We visited the stores of lacquered ware and china ware, and also shops containing silk and cotton goods. Their products are fair. Strangers have to change their Mexican silver dollars at their custom house into the silver coin of their country, in order to buy the least thing. Well, what shall I say of the Japanese? They beat all my comprehension. No nation are like them. Their streets are clean and neat. Military stations are frequent, and double-sword officers are constantly passing by. But the customs of the people are antagonistic to our own as much as possible. For instance, we visited in our walks, public bath-houses, where men and women, old and young, were promiscuously bathing together. Not as at Cape May or Newport, but lacking the bathing dress. I infer that the law of decency or virtue is unknown here except after marriage. 'Tis the rule here that females are to have lovers, many or few, until marriage, but if after marriage any dereliction from the marriage vow be proved or be known, the neighbors come in and put an end to the woman. At 3 P.M., to-day, we returned to the ship. I had dinner, and at four took a nap, but the band aroused me, and I wound up the day with a long yarn on deck with Mr. Coolidge. I have a letter of introduction to Dent & Co.'s agents here, but have not presented it; shall do so to-morrow.

October 11th. I have been ashore to-day, and presented my letter of introduction as I proposed, received kindly and invited to visit, &c., &c. I am generally adverse to letters of introduction, and prefer a letter of credit, which is a pretty sure passport anywhere. I have bought here only a piece of eighteen yards of silk, and a piece of twenty yards of crape, intended as material for dressing-gown and lining for your good self; also, two or three dozen cups and saucers of wafer porcelain, to send home. Kanagawa is the place to buy at. I write this to-night, as a vessel leaves for Hong-Kong on Saturday (day after to-morrow), and will probably arrive there in time to place our letters in the out-going mail of Oct. 25th. If my friends expect letters from me, you had better give them this one to read. Give my love to father, the girls and George. We leave here, *via* the inland sea, for Osaca and Kanagawa, in about five days. I cannot say how long I shall stay at the latter place, but probably a fortnight or three weeks, including the expected Jeddo trip, if we find the "Niagara's" party and Japanese Commissioners going up. I trust I shall return to Hong-Kong in this ship, or by sailing vessel, and be there before the latter end of November. If nothing of a business nature keeps me longer, I shall pass only a week or two there, and then push on for the United States and home.

Your affectionate Son,

HENRY.

{ U. S. S. "HARTFORD" AT ANCHOR AMONG
THE ISLANDS AT THE ENTRANCE OF THE
INLAND SEA, ON THE COAST OF JAPAN. }

Wednesday Evening, October 17, 1860.

My very dear Mother:

We left Nagasaki this morning at eight o'clock, and have been running all day under sail and steam, having made, say, one hundred miles. We are bound to Kanagawa, but instead of going outside along the northeast coast, we steer west for one hundred and fifty miles, and then enter a narrow inland sea, and proceed east toward our point. We go this way because no ship of war has yet been through; also, because there are one or two important cities to see, and perhaps touch at, on the way; and also, because 'tis said to excel in the beauty of its scenery, any other passage known. To-day, we have been among islands, and along close into the mainland ; near enough to swim ashore, all most elaborately cultivated; you can form no idea of it from my description. To-night, as we were at tea, joking and enjoying supper, our fine ship struck on a reef twice, and gave us symptoms of immediate shipwreck. We were running at half speed, but with the swell of the sea and impetus of our going, shot us over the reef. Had it been a foot higher, our ship would have been probably lost upon it. No one knows the peculiar sensation of a long heavy ship, like this, striking when you are underway and least expect it. We anchored in ten minutes after, and here we lay for the night. I suppose we shall be seven or eight days going to Kanagawa, as we have to anchor every night. We have two Japanese pilots on board, but they cannot see at night among islands and shoals. We have to-day passed the most remarkable island; it is two hundred feet high, and only sixty feet across at the base, with a hole through it, forming as perfect an arch as ever was built by man. 'Tis volcanic, as are many of the islands you see here. This was evidently a jet of lava thrown up out of the sea, and cooled as it stands. You have no idea how deep the water is, close in with the shore of the islands; it is as perfect blue as it is outside. I think I shall now retire for the night.

October 18th, 8 P.M. This morning at six o'clock I was on deck, and found the watch lifting the anchor while the band was playing for them. It is customary in a man-of-war, for the band to play a lively air when the crew have such work to do; they keep step to it as they use the capstan bars. We were soon on our way again, with a fresh breeze; as the day advanced, it increased to a heavy northwest gale; and after running all day through straits, among beautifully cultivated islands, etc., the wind howling, and sea white as a cotton field, we anchored close to a large city at four this afternoon. We then went ashore in two boats to see the extensive city, not knowing whether the people would allow us to land or not. As we approached in the boats, the whole city front seemed alive with people; we landed and were not molested, though I suppose no foreigner ever set foot there before; a body of police took us in charge, showed us the city, its temples, etc., etc., and watched us and the populace, which thronged the streets, with equal attention. No noise, or talk, or disturbance took place. We threw a few pieces of silver among the crowd, but in one instance it was picked up by the police, and returned to us. They would not, at the shops, sell us anything if they could help it. While writing here, one of our officers has just brought me in a teapot as a present, which he bought on shore at sundown; we came off to the ship, the wind blowing a gale even in this sheltered spot under the highlands, and tide running very strongly. Really our experiment proved a happy one, for we did not know if the people would allow us to come on shore. I shall now leave my letter to relate future progress in after a while. We get our anchor up in the morning so as to start by daylight, or a little after.

You are at once struck with the strict obedience of the people to their superiors and officers. No one seems to venture to a say a word, if a policeman commands silence. Streets are neat and clean; so are the houses. Our interpreter told the chief functionary that we were American officers of a U. S. man-of-war, and merely wished to see their city; the officers had not even side arms. To-day two of the officers told me I must continue their guest in the ship, not only to Kanagawa and Jeddo, but return to Hong-Kong. I, of course, shall be happy to continue in the ship, but it seems like using a friend to avail of such an offer. I expect, however, I shall return to Hong-Kong in her; she is a noble ship. We took (or rather the Commodore took) two more passengers at Nagasaki; the Consul there and a Missionary; both for Kanagawa; the latter speaks Japanese, and he acts as interpreter to the pilots. I expected the captain would want my room for one of them; I offered it, but the old captain said, "No, sir; I gave you the room, and you are to continue to occupy it; these men can sleep where they can best find room." My room is nearly as large as your little front room up stairs, where I used to sleep when a boy. A fine black walnut bedstead, a French mode, a ditto bureau and writing desk, a mirror, curtains and venetians, library and room for two trunks, chair, washstand, etc., etc.; the floor has a nice Brussels carpet upon it, and everything new, of course, because 'tis the ship's first cruise. I cannot understand how it is that I was so fortunate as to have such a conveyance for such a trip. Well, I will write no more until to-morrow. Mr. Coolidge has just looked in, and said good-night.

October 19, 9 P.M. I have been in Charles Downes' room all the evening, he being sick. We again lifted our anchor this morning, and started on our way. We have run all day with a fine, fair wind, through a smooth sea dotted with islands. To-night, at 7 P.M. we dropped anchor between two islands, where we now are at anchor, "laid remote from home." A most remarkable sea is this indeed; one might rather call the passage a long strait. The usual routine has been gone through with—eating, music, quarters, promenading, talking, reading, etc., etc. I cannot realize I am in this quarter of the globe, except when I am on shore. I will defer writing more until to-morrow.

October 20th, Sunday. Were I at home to-day, and at this hour, I should probably be with you at church; but as I am here on board a man-of-war, I will do the next best thing, which is to write you a few lines. We are sailing and steaming along while I write, about seven miles an hour; 'tis a cold, raw, drizzly Sunday morning, but we on board have had a good hot breakfast, and are as comfortable as mice with cheese. Last evening at eight, a boat came off to us from a city, while we were at anchor, having four men who said they had been sent to know if the Prince of the place could send any supplies of firewood or water to us, or if we required anything. We told him no; that we were bound from Nagasaki to Jeddo, etc., etc. These fellows on coming upon the deck, all got upon their knees, and bumped their foreheads upon the deck as a salutation. We showed them all about the ship, and I took them into my room; they seemed amazed at everything they saw. They went into the engine room below, and seemed surprised to see such strange sights as this ship afforded. Just as they were going away, they again asked if nothing could be sent to us. One of us told him in fun, to send us a fish in the morning for each man; he said yes, he could, but he changed his mind, when we told him we had 336 people on board. I shall continue my letter now directed to father.

Your affectionate Son,

HENRY.

{ U. S. S. S. "HARTFORD," Sunday, Oct. 21, 1860. }
{ AT ANCHOR IN THE INLAND SEA OF JAPAN, OFF }
{ THE CITY OF YOGO (OR HIOGO.) }

My very dear Father:

I continue my letter from my mother's. The last few days I have been writing to her, until my sheet is full; and I therefore renew in this, the narrative of my criuse. It is Sunday evening; we have been running all day, but anchored at dark off a city called Yogo, one of the ports named in our treaty to be opeued to us in 1862. I have not seen the place yet, as I was taking a Sunday nap at dark; but directly went on deck, and could only discern through the foggy mist about us, a fleet of junks. I expect to-morrow we shall go ashore for an hour or two; if so, I will on my return, jot down what we saw. I cannot realize that we are here: in a fine, armed ship, with intelligent and able men to care for her by night and day; a table which supplies everything for our fare which this quarter of the world will supply. All that I have to do is to make myself comfortable and agreeable. No such opportunity will soon again fall to the lot of any man to visit these seas and this remarkable country. I have made a mistake in dating my letter to mother all along; it should be one day later, as I find to-day is the 21st instead of the 20th, as I have named in hers.

Tuesday, October 23d. Yesterday morning at daylight, our ship was surrounded by Japanese boats filled with men and women; many of the former came on board; you can have no idea of the curiosity displayed by them. The evening before, our commodore sent his card by some Japanese to be forwarded to the city of Osaca, twenty-five miles farther on; at ten o'clock yesterday we landed. The barge containing the commodore led the way, carrying the ensign in the stern, and the blue flag forward; next came the captain's boat in which I had a seat, and the third boat contained the other officers from the midshipmen's mess. We were received by the police as usual. Our officers had side arms; the police had single swords. We visited temples, stores, etc., and after being ashore two hours, went aboard at noon; got our anchor, and left for Osaca. twenty-five miles. Here we anchored at the mouth of the river, and received during the rest of the day and night, visits from the Japanese. I had supposed that to-day the boats would be manned, and we should go up to this famous city, distant seven miles; but while I was dressing this morning, I heard the orderly walk in and speak to the captain through his door—"the commodore desires steam as soon as possible, and the ship got underway." I expect the old gentleman was angry with the Japanese for having taken so little notice of his coming; at any rate, while I write it is noon, and we are just emerging from the inland sea and the anchorage off Osaca, out upon the open sea on the coast of Niphon, bound up to Kanagawa, the seaport of Jeddo, distant three hundred miles; we are steaming from eight to nine knots. I trust we shall return to Osaca, as it is important that these Japanese may not be led to think that by our going away we were afraid to land. Osaca is a city of seven to eight hundred thousand people or more; it is a third one in the empire, contains many extensive palaces and temples, and should be visited by us no doubt. For years it was the residence of the missionaries from Portugal—Jesuits—until their destruction by the Japanese decrees against christianity, in the seventeenth century. Budhism is the religion of the Japanese generally. We saw at Yogo or Hiogo, some of the largest men I ever saw. October 24th, 7 P.M. Sixty miles distant from Kanagawa. We are steaming up the bay which leads to Kanagawa. Yesterday afternoon we got out into open sea, upon the coast, a blowy, drizzly day; at night the wind increased, and we realized by the lurching of the ship and the piping of the wind, the truth of the stories which are told of the weather here. By 10 P.M., the ship was going thirteen knots, and the wind blowing a gale. At 11 P.M., the Japanese pilot desired the ship kept out farther from the coast, as he said reefs made out a long way; of course we steered as he directed. We got roughly handled, but to-day we got into this bay again, and have been running into smoother water. At eleven this forenoon, we made the mountain of Fusi-Yama, 13,000 feet high; its summit covered with drifted snow—a beautiful sight—as its top peered out above all the cloud, snow-clad, against the clear, blue sky. This afternoon we passed a volcanic island on our starboard hand, which was smoking freely. We have just passed this afternoon the city of Simoada, where in 1858, a Russian frigate was lost with all hands, in an earthquake in the harbor. This city lies near the foot of the mountain I referred to. You cannot conceive the relief it is to be on an even keel again, after being pitched and rolled about in a blow; another thing about it is, that these seas are none too well surveyed; and on a volcanic coast like this, one might find land in open sea. Well I will leave this now, until we reach Kanagawa.

Sunday, 28th Oct., at Kanagawa, U. S. Consulate. Here I am living with E. M. Dorr, consul here, at his residence in Kanagawa. We arrived on the 25th. Dorr came on board that evening, officially, to call on the commodore, and urged me to go to his house that evening, but I did not until next day. On the 26th I landed here with the commodore, captain, the flag-lieutenant and Mr. Coolidge; called on Dorr and three missionary families, and took up my room here. Dorr has the best house in Japan. You cannot imagine how oriental everything about it appears.

I intended to have gone on board the "Hartford" to-day, to attend service, but owing to a rain storm, I abandoned it, knowing that no service would be held. Kanagawa is in the bay of Jeddo, occupied only by the Japanese, say 80,000, and the consuls of the three treaty powers. Trade is carried on at Yokahama, four miles below ; no merchant can live at Kanagawa. Dorr lives in an old temple converted into a fine house. Six missionary families also live close to the consuls. The country is perfection; soil rich and most elaborately cultivated. I have been the past two days over to Yokohama—every morning about ten, and return at 3 P.M., to make purchases. The display of goods there is really worth seeing. I met many friends over there who offered me rooms and *chow-chow*, if I would stay with them. I met yesterday the Dutch and English consuls and French minister at the house of the Dutch consul.

Thursday, 1st Nov., 12 M. Here we are at anchor six miles distant from the city of Jeddo, that immense city, which so few Europeans have ever to this day beheld. We can approach no nearer with our ship, owing to want of water. On our port side lies the Prussian frigate, "Arcona," and on the starboard the Prussian frigate, "Thetis"; the former the flag-ship of the minister who is trying to negotiate a treaty with the Japanese. But I must go back a little. Last Tuesday evening, at Kanagawa,. the Dutch consul and two of our lieutenants dined at Dorr's. Wednesday, the commodore had a reception at Dorr's at noon, and sixty people, principally Americans, came. We had a feast, dancing, &c., until six P.M., when the visitors dispersed. We then had a quiet dinner party among ourselves, consisting of Dorr, the commodore, his flag-lieutenant and myself; also, the doctor or surgeon. At 10 P.M., we left the commodore to go to bed, and took the band to go serenading. Imagine us going through streets with sixteen lantern-bearers before us, each lantern being a transparency on a pole, striped alternate red and blue, with the stars on one side and the eagle on the other, representing the American flag; then ourselves, then the band playing and then about 5,000 Japanese, principally women, all perfectly delighted and blocking up the road as far as we could see back. With this escort we went to the English consul, then to the French minister, then to the missionaries, especially to one place to serenade a young lady, a daughter of a missionary. We got through at midnight. At seven the next morning, I took a boat for the ship, and at nine, we were off for the city of Jeddo. In three hours we reached the

city front, where we now lay, four miles distant. I
did not go on shore that day, being too far to pull
up and back; but yesterday I went. Of course, to describe the city, I cannot. It is, I judge, some fifteen
or twenty miles long by six miles deep, and contains
anywhere from five to ten millions of people; nearer
ten than five, I should say. We went to a hill in the
city, from which we took a survey over its whole extent. The palace of the Tycoon emperor is in the
centre of the city, surrounded by two walls, and covering about as much area as Boston Common, say
forty acres; the whole is surrounded by a broad
moat. The city residences of the Damioes, or heredi-
tary princes, are all over the city, and occupy much
ground. Its temples are very numerous, and placed
on all the hills and most beautiful spots. Some parts
of the city are magnificent, fine, wide roads to ride
over and ample room, while in other sections, narrow
streets and a denseness of people render walking or
riding alike disagreeable. The people seem well dis-
posed, but still the soldiers and followers of the Damioes often are to be met inflamed with *sacke,* (or wine
made from rice), and these are most hostile towards all
foreigners. We leave for Kanagawa to-morrow morning, to-day being Sunday, the 4th—and we leaving to-
morrow makes five days which we have been at anchor here. We are to touch at Kanagawa for a day,
and then proceed to Hong-Kong. Commodore Stribling, his flag lieutenant and Mr. Coolidge left the ship
when we were at Kanagawa, and rode up to Jeddo by
land and took up quarters at Mr. Harris', the minister. Dorr offered me a horse to make one of this
party, which had I accepted, I suppose I should have

stayed at Harris'; but I preferred to come up by ship,
only twelve miles. All together, this cruise so far has
been so novel, so pleasant, so full of interest and accomplished in so short a time, as to render it quite an
event in my experience, and one which I would not
have missed for a great deal of money. Let me advise
you to purchase "Hildreth's Japan," an authentic and
quite a reliable book, full of interest and fact. I have
written this letter to mother and yourself most care-
lessly, at all hours, in all places, and under all circum-
stances of smooth and rough weather, badly punctu-
ated and unfit to be read except by those at home, who
make allowance for my mistakes under such circum-
stances. I shall leave it now to attend Divine Service
on deck. Oh! I find 'tis raining; so we are at home,
no service. The city of Jeddo, seven years ago, was
one-fourth destroyed, with one-fourth its entire popu-
lation,' by an earthquake. They visit this place regu-
larly every seven years. I presume nowhere in the
world are they more severe.

Tuesday, the 6th, 7 p.m., at sea. We left Jeddo
yesterday, at 9 a.m., and anchored at Kanagawa in
three hours after. I passad last night on shore at
Dorr's, dined there, where I met at dinner the commodore of the Prussian squadron, our consul from Haka-
dadi and the interpreter at the legation of the U.S. at
Jeddo. After dinner, say at midnight, I retired, and
arose this morning at seven, took a boat at once and
reached our ship at eight—our hour for sailing being
nine. We left this morning about eleven o'clock, and
are now steaming and sailing for Hong-Kong. We have
just got out of the bay, I believe, into open sea. Passed
a volcanic island to-day, which was smoking at its

crater. Mr. Coolidge is still on board. Yesterday, as
we were coming from Jeddo to Kanagawa, we met the
U. S. dispatch boat, "Saganaw," with the mails from
Hong-Kong for this ship. She reports the "Niagara"
at Hong-Kong. We have just missed her. We may
meet her to-morrow, as she is now eight days out from
there, bound up here. I received no letters, as I or-
dered them kept at Hong-Kong. The Dutch bark,
which Edward Gassett took passage in for Kanagawa,
was wrecked seven days out from Hong-Kong, and·
poor Gassett was nine days in a boat on four spoons-
full of water a day. I wrote you some time ago that
he asked me to go with him, and that I would have
gone had I been at liberty, but, having a little business,
I could not get off in time, so I took steamer to Shanghai, instead of beating up in his bark.

7th Nov., 8 P.M. I was wrong in writing yesterday
that we had run out of the bay and were in open sea,
We took a north-west gale yesterday at 4 P.M., and
tumbled about all night, rolling and plunging fright-
fully among islands and reefs, not correctly laid down
on charts. 'Twas the worst night I have ever seen at
sea, I think; even our good commodore was on deck
a great deal during the night. Fortunately it was
moonlight. It has not moderated much yet, having
been blowing now for twenty-four hours, but the ship
is easier. I got no sleep last night, but took three hours
in cat naps to-day. Even now while I write, the ship
is rolling, a high, turbulent sea running, three double-
reefed topsails and a foresail, is about the bulk of our
canvas. Weather cold and clear. I shall leave you
now to try and get a nap.

Sunday evening, 11th November. I left writing four days ago, just after a gale of wind. I resume now just after another. For the last two days we have had bad weather. Last night we were again among islands to the north of the Lew Chew, or Loo Choo group; wind howling and a tremenduous sea, besides not having had an observation, we could not tell exactly our position. We rolled last night so that I could not sleep, but had enough to do to keep in my bed and not fall out. To-day has been clear, and we have been running from nine to thirteen knots an hour, going like a race horse; rolling sometimes the lee and then the weather guns under water. We passed four miles from an island 2000 feet high, to-day — an extinct volcano — a regular crater at its top. You would laugh at the idea of any one writing, if you could see how the ship rolls now. We have run from Kanagawa eight hundred miles, and have nine hundred more to go before reaching Hong-Kong. We want to get in by the 15th, on which day the mail leaves, but I fear we shall hardly do it, as it requires us to make ten miles an hour night and day from now until Thursday morning, (four days).

My last letter to you was written at Nagasaki, and sent from there about the 15th of October to Hong-Kong, and should have gone to you per overland mail on 25th last month. I trust it went all right. That letter, with this long one, will give you an account of my whereabouts since leaving Shanghai. We have just found out on board that the commodore intends taking this ship to Siam and then to Manila, soon after arriving at Hong-Kong, and I am requested to continue my trip to those places. But the fact is, I want to see home; and as I think the "Niagara" will take Mr.

Ward as far as Aden, I shall try to go in her if I get the opportunity. However, I can tell better after our arriving in Hong-Kong. 'Tis certainly a rare opportunity of seeing these two places, and I should be happy to continue my cruise longer in the ship. I do not know when Mr. Coolidge intends going home. We take a constitutional walk together daily. He knows Boston people well. He asked me to-day what I intended doing on arriving home. I told him, " go into some business connected with this quarter of the world, so as to be employed and making money."

You should have seen this ship at noon to-day. Her great length and fine proportions under short sail, diving bows under, then a roll, then another dive, as if she could not go fast enough; sea fairly boiling, sun out bright after the storm; water tumbling in occasionally over our rails. I think I never saw finer sailing, more majestic, rather, though I have seen quieter. Take your map and you can see our position, running from the Pacific into the China Sea, through a group of islands between the Loo Choo Islands on the south of us and coast of Japan or Van Diemen's straits to the north of us. Then turn to Jeddo Bay, Japan, and you can see our track. I have some beautiful things from Japan. Among them is a crystal eighteen inches in circumference, without a flaw, clear as the air or the purest spring water. It was taken from a cave in Japan, made into a perfect sphere in form, by artificial means, and is pronounced by Mr. Coolidge and by our officers, as well as by foreigners in Japan, something never seen before, not even in the best cabinets in Europe.

November 13th, 7 P.M. I resume my letter, though the ship is running under sail alone, very fast, and yielding to the sea by rolling, though not so heavily as when I left this letter.

Last evening Mr. Coolidge and myself took tea with the midshipmen, and passed a pleasant evening. I know of nothing more refreshing than, when tired of all one sees about them, especially in a ship at sea, to retire to the privacy of his own apartment and write a letter home. The longer I meditate upon going home, the stronger becomes my resolution to do so, and I think now the inducement which would keep me in China any longer, would be a rare one indeed. I feel alone in the world, though surrounded with friends, and I expect I shall never quite cure that until I have a wife. I shall, at once on arriving at Hong-Kong, make preparation to leave it for home. We ought to be in there now, say day after to-morrow evening, if the present rate of speed is kept up. I cannot tell you how delightful this trip has been, from the day I left Hong-Kong to the present, especially when I embarked in this ship, then our passage through the inland sea, the fine weather we there experienced, absence of fogs, the novelty attaching to all we saw, my stay on shore at Kanagawa at Dorr's, for a week, our trip to Jeddo, in fine, the whole ; even the subsequent bad weather at sea had its advantage, for it gave a greater degree of delight to the days of fine sailing.

This ship rolls terribly. We have the wind now right behind us, or " dead aft," and she always rolls worse when sailing with the wind there. My visit at Jeddo was, of itself, of no slight privilege. No merchants · are allowed to go. The residents of

Kanagawa and Yokohama (foreigners), though but twelve miles distant from the Imperial City, cannot visit it. But I, being in a government ship, could wear side arms and the button, and consequently, with the officers, enjoyed what I could not have seen had I gone to Kanawaga in a sailing ship. No merchant ship of any nation can go to Jeddo, or above Kanagawa or Yokohama. I told Mr. Coolidge to-day I would like to make the same trip over again at once.

As I have once or twice already remarked in this letter, we are hoping to reach Hong-Kong before the mail steamer leaves on the 15th, at 2 P.M., we must run ten miles an hour from now up to that time, to do it. I think we shall accomplish it, though our officers think not. I am writing this letter to go by it, so if we get in only half an hour before the mail goes, this may go by it. I will leave this space now to add some-thing by and by, either just as we reach Hong-Kong or before. We are now off the north end of Formosa. bound down the sea.

15th November, 9 A.M. We have just had prayers on deck, and I have returned to my room to add a few lines to my letter. We are now fifty miles distant only from an anchorage, and unless we run that distance before two o'clock to-day, we shall miss the mail. I think we shall accomplish it. I should regret losing by an hour to send letters this mail. I will close this now, and trust to its going forward by this day's steamer. Give my kind regards to friends about you. I trust that I shall have the pleasure of seeing you in a few months, at farthest. Until then believe me your affectionate and obedient son and servant,

H. P. BLANCHARD.

Having an invitation from his Excellency, John E. Ward to join him upon his return from China, until he reached his family in Europe, I accepted his appointment, so kindly made to me, of Secretary to the Legation. On Saturday morning, December 15th, 1860, I left my residence at Hong-Kong at a quarter before 8 A.M. and went on board the U. S. S. S. "Hartford" to breakfast with and take farewell of her officers; the captain and commodore with whom I had so recently passed two months, upon a most delightful cruise to Japan. At 9.30 P.M., Mr. Ward, came to pay his parting call to the commodore; and at 10 A.M., I left with Mr. Ward in the barge for the U. S. S. F. "Niagara," which ship lay just ahead. As we got clear of the "Hartford," she fired a salute of twenty-one guns; her yards were manned, as were also those of the "Niagara." In five minutes we were alongside and on board the "N," which ship commenced her salute also of twenty-one guns. 'Twas soon over; the order was immediately given "up anchor," and by 10.15 A.M., this huge ship was steaming out of harbor toward the Luy-e-Moon passage. The spacious cabin occupied by Mr. Ward and myself, has eight large staterooms with every fitting for elegance and comfort. In the rear are two large bathing rooms, etc., and the whole is flush with the upper or main deck. By noon we were fairly at sea, experiencing an ugly sea with an unpleasant roll of the ship. At 3 P.M. we dined with the captain in his spacious saloon below our own; Colonel Ripley being at table, he having come out in the ship for the government. Mr. Buchannan, captain's clerk, was also at the table. The band played during dinner; the captain entertained us handsomely, while the ship was, by this time, running before a strong northeast monsoon, twelve miles per hour under sail. We, this day, triced up our propeller, it being useless in a strong breeze. Tea was served at seven, but neither Mr. Ward or myself cared to attend, having dined heartily; at 10 P.M. retired. Sunday, the 16th, the wind continued, and at twelve to-day, we have run 274 miles. Divine service was held to-day by Mr. Stuart, the chaplain, on the berth deck; all hands present; read and slept the rest of the day; at 9 P.M., retired.

Monday, 17th. Wind light; ship rolls a good deal; carrying lower studding-sails. At twelve noon had run two hundred and thirty-one miles the last twenty-four hours; altered our course from southeast to southwest, having passed Macclisfield Bank at 4 P.M. Dined at three with the captain; Mr. Brown, the first Lieutenant present The ward-room mess consists of fifteen excellent and efficient gentlemen. I have been in to see them several times already. The band played several pieces during dinner, and also after dinner, upon the quarter deck. This P.M. the guns were run out and exercised; afterwards a prayer by the chaplain; retired at 10 P.M.

Tuesday. Wind light; run up to 12 A.M. to-day, for twenty-four hours, one hundred and fifty-six miles; had steam got up and propeller lowered at 9 P.M.

Wednesday. With steam and canvas to-day, run up to 12 M. for twenty-four hours, one hundred and eighty miles; at 4 P.M. saw an immense water spout, distant four miles; also passed an English ship with troops, steering south, and another ship steering southeast; could not discern her colors. Weather squally toward evening, but last part, wind light.

Thursday. Squally, with much rain; distance run this day, one hundred and ninety miles. An English ship in company with us all this day steering south-southeast. The band as usual played at dinner; a prayer by the chaplain at 9 A.M., and 5 P.M., after inspection.

Friday, 21st. No wind; under steam, have made to twelve noon, two hundred and twenty miles. Had a pleasant dinner, band playing, etc.; after dinner, a pleasant conversation with Colonel Ripley.

Saturday, Dec. 22d. Steady steaming to-day has run us up to an anchorage off the light-house, at the entrance of Singapore Straits, at 10 P.M., having run to twelve noon this day, two hundred and ten miles. We passed this day, three English transports, bound from China to Singapore, and home.

Sunday, Dec. 23d. To-day, at noon, anchored within two miles of Singapore, after a run of thirty-six miles in from the lighthouse. At 1 P.M. I went on shore with Mr. Ward, our purser. We landed opposite the monument; went to the " Hotel l' Esperance," (formerly the " London Hotel l' Esperance"; had lunch, took a carriage, drove to the news-room, and then to the American Consul's, distant two miles in the country. Here we passed an hour, then drove two or three miles further to a new residence unoccupied, but which commands the best view in Singapore. At sundown we returned to town, and went off to the ship. I was in Singapore five years since, and passed six weeks; 'twas during the prevalence of the southwest monsoon, when frequent rains rendered the country beautiful; whether or no 'twas the difference in the season now which seems to render Singapore less attractive or not, I do not know; but neither the town or the country seem so inviting as when I last visited the place. The building of a fort on the water front, also, of a new church, and a few new residences has somewhat improved the architectural appearance of the town.

Monday, Dec. 24th. The American Consul break-fasted with us. We gave the town a salute of twenty-one guns this morning at eight o'clock ; then at nine fired nine guns for the Consul, and at 9.30 A.M., got underway for Aden; at twelve, noon, we met the U. S. Steamer ''Dacotah,'' from the U. S. *via* the Cape and Ceylon. She rounded too and sent us a mail bag for the '' Niagara;'' after being alongside twenty minutes, she steamed on to Singapore, while we in time, pursued our course. The ''Dacotah'' is one of the E. I. Squadron,'' and bound to China. Our band played several airs; among them, '' Sweet Home''; which, after an absence like mine, of five years, one can understand, would have some effect.

The weather for several days has been quite hot, calling into use our white pants, jackets and coats. Saw two vessels to-day, a bark and brig, standing through the straits toward Singapore. We are this day running under steam. To-morrow, being Christmas, I have an invitation to dine with the wardroom officers.

December 25th, Christmas day. We are to-day, using steam, running through the straits of Malacca, and expect to pass Penang to-morrow, at 6 A.M. Our boilers are bad, and our chief engineer says we may not be able to run with them all the way to Aden. I fear our coal will give out; and if it is decided that we cannot go into Galle with this ship, 'twould seem the part of prudence to coal at Penang, as our supply of black diamonds does not now exceed 500 tons. We use thirty-three tons per day. Jardine's Steamer "Lancefield" from China for Calcutta, passed us this morning. Weather hot—the Malacca shore in sight all the time. At three this P.M., in company with his Excellency, Mr. Ward, Captain McKean and Colonel Ripley, of the army, I dined at the wardroom mess; twenty composed the dinner party. We rose at 6 P.M., after a delightful dinner, which was well served and enjoyed the more, because accompanied by the band, which played for us. To-night, at sundown, six or eight square-rigged vessels are in sight. We passed the light-ship at noon; distance run, two hundred and ten miles to twelve noon, to-day.

December 26th, Wednesday. This morning at seven o'clock, we made a brig and bark at anchor twenty-six miles from Penang laden with coolies. In running ahead of the latter, but too close to her, not making allowance for tide which was setting us upon her, we carried away her bowsprit and stove our larboard boats. We then run around her, asked if she wished a tow into Penang, to which he replied, "yes." We again fouled her by running alongside; at length we took her in tow, 3 P.M. We have towed the bark into port, or rather just off the port of Penang; paid her owner who was on board $1,000 damages, which settled the difficulty amicably. The vessel had a Chinese captain and an English mate; the owner was a Cingalese. We are now steering for a point to clear Acheen Head, on the north end of Sumatra; no wind, and only under steam. Had music this afternoon, and prayers as usual.

Thursday, December 27th. Steaming seven and a half knots per hour, no wind, weather hot, bound over to Acheen Head; distance run to twelve noon, to-day, one hundred and ninety miles.

Friday, 28th December. This A.M. at eight, passed Acheen Head, steering west-by-north; a light breeze; running under steam and sail.

Saturday, December 29th. We lost sight of the Island of Nicobar to the northward of Acheen Head, yesterday evening, and to-day are running seven knots per hour under canvas alone, with propeller triced up. This Island of Nicobar seems to be some twenty miles square; luxuriant growth of woods, etc. upon it, and undoubtedly a rich island in gums, woods, precious stones, etc., etc. No signs of inhabitants, but 'tis peopled with the race which inhabit also the Andamans. We passed this island on our starboard beam.

Sunday, 30th December. Light breeze, propeller triced up, sailing seven knots; weather fine, with an occasional squall; distance this twenty-four hours, one hundred and thirty-five miles to twelve noon. Had divine service to-day.

Monday, December 31st. A fair breeze, wind east-northeast; distance run to-day at noon, one hundred and sixty-five miles, under canvas.

Tuesday, January 1, 1860. Under sail only; running eight to nine knots toward Ceylon—twelve noon, land of Ceylon in sight, having run the last twenty-four hours, two hundred and ten miles. We do not touch, but proceed direct to Aden.

Wednesday, 2d. Strong winds all day; at night a fresh gale from north. Steaming and sailing, distance run, two hundred miles; course, northwest.

Thursday, 3d. Propeller triced up at nine this A.M. Wind light, Cape Cormorin in sight this A.M. Steaming all this day; wind west at sundown. We ran two hundred miles the last twenty-four hours to noon, to-day.

Friday 4th. To twelve this noon, have run one hundred and ninety miles, being now sixteen hundred and eighty miles from Aden. Steaming seven knots, no wind. This evening passed the Island of Minacor; people thereon said to be friendly. This evening triced up propeller, having a four-knot breeze.

Saturday, January 5th, 8 A.M. Lowered propeller again, having no wind. Yesterday we ran about one hundred and eighty miles. To-day, at twelve noon, our run for the last twenty-four hours will have been less, as we have laid still all night.

Sunday, January 6th. A charming day; a long prosy sermon at 10.30 A.M. Ship steaming eight knots. "Oh! when will all our wanderings end." Distance run to twelve noon, to-day, two hundred miles.

Monday 7th. Still steaming on through an almost motionless and waveless sea. Now and then a few sea birds are seen hovering over a school of fish, but little else can we discern to break the monotony of the voyage. A daily review of the marines and exercise of guns and seamen, afford us some variety, while sleeping, reading and conversing, with eating and drinking, fills up the remainder of our time.

Tuesday 8th. Distance run to-day, to noon, one hundred and seventy-eight miles, under steam alone.

Wednesday, 9th. Still steaming; no wind since leaving Ceylon; distance one hundred and seventy miles.

Thursday. Steaming; distance to noon, one hundred and seventy-eight miles.

Friday morning, ten o'clock. Made the island of Socotra, and have run alongside of it all the latter part of this day on the northern edge; distance one hundred and sixty miles to noon.

Saturday 12th. This day ran one hundred and eighty miles under steam and sail.

Sunday. Another long prosy sermon about nothing at all. Distance run to-day, one hundred and ninety-eight miles up to twelve noon.

Monday, January 14th. An unfortunate fireman lost his life to-day, by a block falling on his head. At 2 P.M. to-day, we anchored at Aden.

ADEN, Tuesday, 15th January, 1861.

We arrived yesterday. The mail from the U.S. reports the election of Abraham Lincoln as President. This morning we buried, at sunrise, the man who was killed yesterday. I went on shore, had a dinner with Captain Webb, who is an agent of Mr. Bertram, of Salem, here. Staid at the hotel during the night ; passed the evening at Captain Thomas', agent of P. & O. Company.

Wednesday. In the evening rode with Captain Mc-Kean of the "Niagara" out to the camp, five miles from the point. Called on Colonel Playfair, the chief official in the place ; stopped and heard the band for quarter of an hour, and rode in again through the fortifications. Passed the evening playing whist at Captain Thomas', with several others. Staid all night at the hotel.

Thursday 17. A party of ladies visited the " Niagara" where we had dancing on deck. Friday another party of ladies came off at Mr. Ward's invitation, he having agreed to meet them on shore, but being ill, I received them in his stead at the landing. All seemed delighted with the noble ship, and with their reception. This evening, in company with a few officers, I went on shore, and serenaded with our band one or two ladies at Captain Thomas'.

Saturday 19. Last night the steamer "Norna" came in from Mauritius, and this morning, at eight, the "Orissa" from Bombay. I took a boat and went on shore to breakfast with Captain Webb, and find we leave per "Orissa" for Suez, to-night, at 8 P.M. At 2 P.M., I returned to our ship, and at 5 P.M. Mr. Ward and myself left our beautiful vessel, her yards manned, band playing, and a salute of twenty-one guns. After so much comfort as we had taken on board that wonderful ship, how could we have left her without feelings of the deepest regret. At sundown, we were on board the P. & O. Company's steamship " Orissa," mixed up with men, women and children, officers of the Queen's army, officers of the E. I. Company's army, sick and well, Arabs, Hindoos, Jews and Somaulis, surrounded with boxes of merchandise, baggage, etc., etc. At 10 P.M. up came the anchor, and we steamed out of port and just by our " Niagara."

I have enjoyed my stay at Aden very much indeed. Captain Webb being there, and living with him on shore, enhanced the pleasure. With him I rode daily, visited ladies, or drove his horse and buggy. The most wonderful thing for visitors at Aden to behold, are the tanks—one of which holds five millions of gallons—constructed by the Arabs centuries ago.

Sunday January 20th. While writing, we have entered the Red Sea and passed the island of Perim, now held by the English. With a fair wind, we are running off our twelve miles per hour.

Aden has a garrison now of fifteen hundred European and Seapoy troops. Coffee trade is carried on here. The Arabs here are fierce and wild, and no foreigner can land upon an adjacent shore without being shot. The Ishmaelite character is fully perceptible. We are now steaming up the Red Sea for Suez. Our party which left the " Niagara," consists of Mr. Ward, Colonel Ripley, Dr. Woodsworth and myself.

January 21st. Our fair wind is now dying gently away, and our captain predicts head winds. Passengers are all well and jolly.

January 22d. The land of Abyssinia is in sight. I omitted to say that on the twentieth we passed in sight of Mocha, where three foreign vessels were at anchor. To-day we have Jidda, the seaport of Mecca, on our starboard side.

January 23rd. Wind strong ahead, blowing down the sea; the shore of Egypt and Arabia on either side, within eight miles.

January 24th. A furious gale last night, but our steamer behaved well, and ran seven miles an hour into the teeth of it.

January 25th. Mt. Horeb and Mt. Sinai in sight on our right hand, being a part of a range of mountains near to us, which are very high and covered with snow.

No one can conceive of the desolation which surrounds that shore, presenting only decaying and decomposing mountains, with their peaks far above the clouds, surrounded by wastes of sand. To be cast away on these shores, is certain death at the hands of the Arabs. These facts, together with the cold at this season, renders the " *tout ensemble*" far from a pleasant locality. The navigation of the Red Sea at this part is narrowed down to but three miles of channel; coral reefs running out on both sides. To-night, at 9 P.M., we passed over the passage of the Israelites when pursued by the Egyptians. At 10.30 P.M. we anchored off the town of Suez. I won the lottery which it is customary to get up upon these steamers on the passage on the minute of arrival, say twenty-five rupees.

January 26th. This morning at half past nine, a steam tug-boat came alongside our steamer, and took all our passengers with their baggage to town. We saw Moses' Well near the bank of the sea as we steamed up. Suez is a mean place, and only Arabs, Jews and camels are seen here. The town is five miles from our anchorage. The railroad which connects Suez with Alexandria, passing through Cairo, comes down upon the wharf. Here we took the cars at once on reaching shore, and at 11.15 A.M., we left Suez for Cairo and Alexandria, over the vast desert where nought save an unlimited waste of sand was visible. Occasionally we passed a few Arab houses, or caves constructed underground. We procured a few biscuits at two way-stations, and after running six hours over this illimitable plain of sand, with no green thing in sight, we suddenly came upon the border of the Nile, and Cairo with its myriad mosques, minarets, cultivated fields, green trees and gardens, rose upon the sight. Such a contrast I never experienced, nor can it be realized save here. We had run ninety miles. We dined at Cairo, and at six the same evening, resumed our rail travel for Alexandria, running over a level country, crossing the Nile twice, and beneath the influence of a matronly moon. As we rode into Cairo, those mighty monuments of antiquity, the three pyramids, rose upon our sight. No one can behold these without reflecting upon the ages which have passed away since their founders flourished, and still there their tombs stand, defying time and guarding the desert. We reached Alexandria at 2 A.M. of the 27th, cold, chilled through and weary with our long, dry, dusty ride over the desert. At the depot, we were received by the acting United States Consul, who had a carriage and a dragoman in waiting, and with whom we went to the Hotel l'Europe. By four this morning we went to bed, but sleeping in wet sheets gave both Mr. Ward and myself a severe cold, from which I anticipate a protracted indisposition. After a poor rest of four hours, I arose, and after riding about, visiting the Exchange, seeing Pompey's Pillow and Cleopatra's Needle, we left Alexandria this day per P. & O. steamer "Ellora," at noon.

January 27th. We left Alexandria in company with the steamer for Marseilles. January 28th. This morning weather fine. Our number of passengers has been pleasantly increased, a Mr. Crockett of Boston, with a number of Americans who have been up the Nile. January 29th. A few vivid flashes of lightning last evening, betokened a storm. This morning, before daylight, it was upon us. The rolling of the ship became severe, and frequent seas fell upon us, taking our life-boat away from the davits, darkening our skylights and pouring down tons of water through our upper-deck hatches. Deeming it imprudent at 10 A.M., to run the ship longer, the sea increasing and now having become fearful, the captain wisely hove her too. We laid all day with the worst sea running which I have ever seen. At sundown it moderated, and glad were we all to look over the crest of the waves toward our haven, and see our steamer underway once more. 30th January, smooth sea. January 31st. At daylight this A.M., we anchored in quarantine harbor, Valetta, Malta. After breakfast we bid adieu to our passengers, two of whom I much regretted leaving, the wife of a major in H. M. Indian army, Mrs. Aitken and a beautiful boy of four years, and a Capt. Douglass of the same army, son of Gen. Sir Jas. Douglass, G. C. B. Here we took rooms at Dunsford's Hotel. February 1st. This day we drove out to the grotto of St. Paul, where he lived for four months after his shipwreck. A church stands upon this spot. The priest who opens to you the descent to this remarkable cave, tells you with the utmost gravity and sincerity that people have carried away ship loads of this cave, but it never grows any larger. Also that when Paul preached here he was distinctly heard in Sicily. We next visited the old Saracenic Catacombs which once led six miles into Valetta, but now are filled up. Next we saw the statue of St. Paul upon the spot where he preached, now a garden of the church. Next the spot where Paul was shipwrecked. After this the old cathedral which was built by one of the grand masters of the celebrated order of the Knights of St. John of Jerusalem. This cathedral is full of old paintings, of beautiful mosaics, and of tombs of bishops beneath the mosaic floor. Upon our return to Valetta we visited the summer palace of the governor, where, upon the trees in the grounds, hung two or three ship loads of lemons and oranges. Next we went to the "College of the Mediterranean," where some seventy students from all parts of Europe and Asia receive European education. The accomplished tutor informed us that the expenditures of this institution exceeded the receipts by £2,500 sterling per annum; which amount he receives from the charities of the nobility of England. We returned to Valetta this evening, after a long and interesting drive. I omitted to say that Mr. Ward, the consul, Mr. Winthrop of Boston and myself called on the governor, where we found at this palace a superb collection of paintings, superb mosaic floors and many suits of armor, one of which was worn by the Knight of the order of St. John, who founded Valetta. Next we were introduced into the library or news room. This evening I procured a box at the opera, where Mr. Ward, Mr. Crockett, myself, an English officer and lady attended. The performance of the prima donna was creditable in the opera of "The Barber of Seville." (Rossini). February 2nd. Visited the church of St. John with its superb oil paintings, its four hundred richly wrought mosaic tombstones, composing its floors, the room beneath the church where repose in marble sarcophagi the dust of the seven grand masters of the knights who built the seven palaces and seven churches, which are to-day the glory of Malta. Doubtless this church is unsurpassed by any other in the world.

February 2nd. Went out to a church of Capuchin friars or monks, where we were shown underneath it, a double row of twenty-six monks, each standing in a niche, dressed in a black gown, the only covering for the skeleton. These grinning, ghastly spectacles have stood in upright posture for from five to fifty years, prevented only from falling by a bar of wood passed around the arms. The main and wonderful features of Malta are its immense forts and fortifications, which must be seen to be appreciated, as no description can afford a faint idea of their magnitude. A garrison of 8,000 English troops hold this island, which is a perfect gem in the circle of islands around it. February 3d, at noon, we embarked on board the *Messagaries Imperiales* steamer, "Porsillippo," bound to Leghorn. We saw Gozo, where Calypso's grotto is, as we passed out by the island. We are to touch at Messina, Naples, and Civitta Vecchia, before reaching Leghorn. Among our passengers is the family of the Earl of Albermarle, consisting of himself, lady Albermarle and their two daughters, the Lady Alice and Lady Louisa Keppel. The Earl is a peer of England, but a most unassuming, plain, charming gentleman. We have a smooth sea and prospect of being at Messina to-morrow. February 4th. Arrived at Messina this morning at daylight. Nothing to see on shore. City occupied by Sardinian troops, while the forts in the harbor are held by the Neopolitan troops. The American steam sloop "Richmond," flag-officer Bell, lies here. I took breakfast with him this A M. To-day he has been on board our steamer to see Mr. Ward, who has been ill below in his stateroom. At 2 P.M. to-day, we left Messina for Naples. To-night at 6 P.M.

we passed Stromboli, rising from the sea, yet showing upon its top its flaming embouchure. At 4 to-day we passed through the straits of Scylla and Charybdis.

February 5th, at 6 A.M., we steamed up the harbor of Naples. The mountain of Vesuvius rose clear against the blue heavens as we passed it, emitting a sluggish cloud of smoke from its crater. On our port side the adjacent country of Naples presented its picturesque scenery of hillsides and slopes crowned with residences. At 9 A.M. we dropped anchor, and at 10 A.M. Mr. Ward and myself went on shore. The police station responded to our application for a pass, "that the Minister of the United States needed none to go wherever he liked." Could the narrow-minded politicians of our beloved country feel and know the real worth of an American citizenship, they would not have led us into this terrible juncture, where only the providence of God can save us from total annihilation. We took a carriage, and after visiting the strada Toledo, the most celebrated street in Europe, the museum and the Consul, we drove through the tunnel and around the drive which is some two miles beyond, and returning by the sea, near the foreign residences. At 4 P.M. we sailed, and blessed with a smooth sea, we passed a quiet night, and at daylight, February 6th, anchored before Civitta Vecchia. Here we delivered most of our passengers, including the Earl and his family. I went on shore, but what with an uninteresting town occupied by French troops, and a rainy day, I was glad to return to the steamer. At 4 P.M. we left.

February 7th. At daylight this A.M., we arrived at Leghorn from Civitta Vecchia. Here we were met by the United States Vice-Consul, who most kindly took us on shore, and was of the utmost aid in passing ourselves and our baggage from the steamer to the cars for Florence. At 9.30 A.M. we left per rail for Florence ; passing through Pisa, the leaning tower in sight ; and after two hours ride through a highly cultivated country, we reached Florence at half past twelve. The most delightful railroad trip I have ever taken; the scenery is very fine, combining natural and artificial attractions. I parted here with my companion, Mr. Ward; he joins his family, who are residing here, while I take rooms in the Hotel de la Ville, but one door removed from him.

23d February. At 4.30 this A. M. I left Florence in the coupé No. 1 of the diligence for Bologna, en route for Venice. I have passed more than a fortnight in Florence, at the Hotel de la Ville, on the Arno; in visiting galleries, palaces and friends, in attending the Opera Bal Masqué, etc. etc., in drives to Fiésole, and over upon the heights on the opposite shore of the Arno. No city in Italy affords attractions for the visitor, or for a resident, which can surpass those of Florence. The city embraces every form of ancient and modern art and architecture. The Pitti Palace, the Uffize, the Corsini, the Boboli Gardens, Fiésole, with its villas and views, the studios—among which Powers' appears in the front rank for works of merit, and Fullers for its Godeva. The cathedral, the churches, in fact everything has a charm for the stranger at Florence. Through Mr. Crockett, a member of the Suffolk Bar of Boston, I met an Italian family, and thus was favored with ingress into Italian society, embracing writers, poets and musical talent, unsurpassed in Italy. Many of my evenings were passed in this society. I also met a Mrs. Fields and daughter, of St. Louis. Three days since, I parted with Mr. Ward, who, with Mrs. Ward, have taken a private carriage or vetturino for Rome, leaving four children behind in care of their niece, Miss Newton, of New York. Well, adieu to Florence. My coupé companions in the diligence prove to be an English lady and daughter, or rather Scotch I infer, though they both drop the H so often, that I found 'twas useless to follow *Punch's* example of picking it up and handing it to them. The mother asking the daughter "which side the Adriatic Naples stood upon?" and the daughter's reply that, "she did not know," gave me a faint idea of the object of their peregrinations. I suppose it to be information. We reached Bologna at 10 P.M. this day, after a hard, but pleasant ride over the Appenines ; and thence over a level road to Bologna. Stopped at Hotel Brun or Suisse.

February 24th, Sunday. This day at noon, I left in a private carriage or vetturino, after visiting the "Academia della Bella Arti," for Ferrara; the two English ladies as my companions. At 7 P.M., we reached the "Hotel d' Europe," after riding all day over a level country, through vineyards all the way. The season is early for vegetation; the weather rainy, and the mountains on all sides covered with snow. Bologna is an interesting, city, presenting miles of corridors as you enter it through its gates. Venice being my destination, I did not remain here.

February 25th. This morning at seven, I again took a seat in the coupé, for Padua, which place, we reached at night, at five o'clock; my English friends still in company, their route being like my own, from Florence to Venice and Paris. We, this day, had our luggage searched as we were entering Austrian dominion; though by right, Austria should relinquish her hold on Venice, Padua, etc., especially since Italy now is united under the rule of Victor Emmanuel. Perhaps, however, Austria is waiting for the French Emperor to withdraw his troops from the Romagna. Six of one and half dozen of the other, I suspect. Here I rested for the dinner hour only; at 9 P.M. we left by rail for Venice. Padua is one of the oldest and most interesting cities of northern Italy. Its streets, squares, cathedrals, etc., etc., are upon a grand-scale, and evince its having seen its days of renown, and merited celebrity. We traveled over most interesting roads from Ferrara to Padua, straight as far as the eye could see, elevated and very solid. One could easily detect that he was within the limit of a powerful sovereign by the innumerable troops to be seen on the roads, and at all the towns and stations " *en passant.*"

At ten this P.M., we arrived at the depot in Venice, after an hour's ride from Padua. I do like the continental arrangement at depots, where guards keep off the crowd, and you are allowed to escape the inconvenience and annoyance of the multitude. We ran for seven miles before entering Venice, over a bridge with the sea on both sides of us. At 11 P.M., we entered a gondola, and started for the Hotel Malberg. After being steered through various little canals by the marvelous dexterity of the gondoliers in the use of one oar, a performance, I believe, unequalled except by the boatman of Venice, we reached the hotel sitsituated upon the Grand Canal.

February 26th. To-day I visited the Palazzo San Marco, the gallery of paintings in the Ducal Palace, the entire palace, the room once occupied by the Council of Ten, the hall where the Inquisitors, three in number, tortured state prisoners, the memorable Bridge of Sighs ; and crossing this, the Infernal Prison, which Byron has long since written of. No wonder when you pass from the Doge's Palace to the solid granite prison, with its grated windows, that sighs escaped the victims who never more saw the light of heaven. A cold chill ran through my frame as I stood upon this memorable spot; and an intimation from the inquisitorial looking gate-keeper who unlocked the iron doors of the prison, and showed me one form of torture, to descend to the dungeons by the light of his greasy candles, was met by me with a positive refusal. God in his infinite mercy forbid in the future history of our globe the re-enaction of scenes such as have been witnessed beneath this "prison, and the palace."

February 26th. I omitted to note at Florence, two important objects of interest which I there enjoyed. One was the celebrated annual carnival, the other the Palace of Prince Demidoff. Of the former, I will only say that the last day of the carnival was lovely, and the Corso unusually attractive. Miles of superb equipages followed successively. Bouquets were thrown from carriage to carriage until sunset, but flour succeeded after dark. I noticed among the most elegant equipages, that of a nephew of the present Emperor of the French, —four bays and gold liveries, a royal turnout. Also the two sons of Victor Emmanuel, with a modest but elegant turnout of one pair silver liveries. A Mr.

Livingstone of New York, six pair of bays. At night, the masked ball was said to have been the best given in Florence for many years. I found the crowd immense on the promenade, while the boxes or loges were also full. Dancing was difficult, owing to numbers. Music, very good. The effect was really unique and exhilarating. Good order until daylight, when the last person left. I had an invite to attend at two boxes, a Mrs. Derby's, of Boston, and Mrs. Crockett; the former through Mrs. Ward.

Next the Palace of Prince Demidoff. The palace, though not the largest, yet I believe is said to be, by the best judges, the gem of all European palaces. Its situation is just outside the walls of Florence, and surrounded by grounds, hot-houses and parks of commensurate richness and extent. To obtain ingress to this palace, requires, usually, a previous application of two months, but through the influence of the Italian ladies to whom I have referred, I was admitted. My good fortune in this respect, was most remarkable, for I am told that there are hundreds of Russian, Italian and Sicilian nobility resident in Florence, who have in vain applied for admission. I can give no just, nor even a faint, description of the treasures of this palace. Its floors and ceilings are of Roman mosaics and Gobelin tapestries. Its mantels of agate, porphyry, lapis-lazuli, and malachite. Its ceilings are hung with superb paintings by Titian, Paul Veronese, Rembrandt, Van Dyke, Leonard da Vinci, and others. Its roofs, especially of the music hall, are of frescoes and gold. Its rooms, successively, are laden with gems, articles of vertu, caskets, silver and gold services, sets of jewels in glass cases, pier tables of Florentine and

Roman mosaic, malachite, etc., etc. Rooms fitted for Turkish occupancy, also for Greeks. A billiard room unsurpassed in the world, the cues studded with jewels. One room filled with pipes of every size, age and value. One filled with ancient armor, one with paintings, in every form of mosaic, one large hall of sculpture, one a gallery of paintings. Beside this, every room having its gorgeous chandeliers and its elaborate furniture, which no pen can describe. After visiting the palace, I walked over the grounds, through the hot-houses, and into the Greek and Catholic chapels attached. Also into the Chinese hall, filled with Chinese antiquities. We passed a day here, and never do I expect to see the same amount of wealth within four walls again. No crowned head of Europe to-day, has anything approaching to it. To visit that palace, would amply repay one for the expense of a voyage from the United States to Europe, and back.

I will now return to the day upon which I made this detour in my narrative. After visiting the square of San Marco, at Venice, watching the flight of pigeons which always arrives there as the clock strikes two, to be fed, I purchased eighteen or twenty views of the city, and returned to the hotel. The church of San Marco, with its enduring mosaics within and without, of gold and brilliant colors, which defy time, its Byzantine style, render it a most imposing and wonderful relic. The scenes portrayed within its walls, upon its roofs, domes and ceilings, in mosaic, are wonderful for beauty and description. Every event of note in our Saviour's life is there portrayed in figures as large as life.

27th February. This day I visited the academy of fine arts, with its galleries of paintings. The palace of the family of Givionelli, where one is shown the remarkable painting of Marino Falieri bidding adieu to his family. We passed to-day the palace of the two Foscari, those of Taglioni (two in number), the once celebrated danseuse, the house where Byron lived when here. I visited the church where are the tombs of Canova and of Titian, each wonderful productions in sculpture. The same church has the tomb of the two Foscari and of Rembrandt.

21st February. To-day I left Venice in company with my recent traveling companions, the English lady and daughter, en route for Paris, by rail. At 10 A.M., we took the cars, and at 5 P.M. reached Milan.

March 1st. Strolled about for an hour or two in shops, and to the celebrated cathedral, which, for its peculiar architecture, surpasses any other in Europe. In the afternoon, I drove to the Place d'Armes, and over the celebrated drive where the Milanese are all found in the public gardens near by, and where the equipages of this beautiful city roll by, each laden with its freight of beauty and of fashion. I have never seen a road so attractive, because so wide, smooth and with a double row of arching shade trees on either hand.

March 2d. Having seen something of Milan, and visited the galleries of paintings and the palace of the King, Victor Emmanuel, I took my passage again per rail, at 11 A.M., to stop at Turin. The ride in the cars is exceedingly attractive and agreeable, as you run over a level country, through many ancient villages and towns, the snow crowned Alps close to you on the right, which separates Piedmont from Savoy. On the left, as you approach Turin, the land is high, and crowned with villas and summer residences of this, hitherto, Piedmontese, but now Italian capital. We crossed through the town of Magenta also, where the recent history of the French interposition points to the renowned field of Magenta.

At 5 P.M., on a cold raw afternoon, we reached Turin, and having accidentally met in the cars two officers, one commanding at Naples, and just returning also from the siege of Gaeta, the other having a military and civil commission, I took a carriage with this latter for his residence and my hotel. I found the Hotel de l'Europe, as is the case with nearly all the best hotels in the middle and south of Europe, in a palace. The room assigned to me was not to my liking, because it was on the third floor; but I was told that the Senate of Italy were then in session, and that most of its members had rooms here, which had completely filled up the house. The dining-room was only sur·passed by that of the hotel where I now am—the Hotel du Louvre. Though it was Sunday, still instead of going to church, I went to picture galleries, the royal palace and the armory. This latter is the best in the world.

In this armory I was shown a lock of hair from the first Napoleon, also the sword which he wore at the sharply contested field of Marengo.

On Monday, the 4th of March, I left the hotel, intending to start again for Paris, but as my trunks were a little behind time, and as the regulations in the railway trains are very severe, I was obliged to return to the hotel and wait another day.

On the 5th, however, at 6.30 P.M., we left, by rail, for the foot of the Alps. At half past eight, we exchanged our comfortable car for a diligence and twelve horses, and began our tedious journey over the Alps, by the pass of Mont Cenis. At 11 P.M., we reached the snow line, and again alighted to exchange our diligence on wheels for one upon runners. By midnight, we had attained such an altitude, as to encounter a furious gale of wind and a temperature of intense cold. The air was filled with dry snow blowing in drifts, so that one could not look to windward. Our road was blocked up with snow, and we continued in this plight until daylight, when we reached the summit, though but for the labors of sixty men who came to dig us out, we would have been there a week. By 1 P.M. of the 6th, we reached a house to dine at in a town on this side the Alps, called Lansleborg. The same evening we arrived at St. Jean de Maurienne, where we passed the night, and took the cars for Paris next day, say March 7th at 6.20 A.M. The scenery is grand by this route over the Alps, but I object to snowdrifts.

March 8th. Having passed all day yesterday, and all night last night in an express train, we reached Paris this morning, at 6.30 o'clock. Smoking is allowed in these cars, and I found it very unpleasant to be shut up with smokers on a cold night. A carriage here conveyed me from the *chemin de fer*, via the Place de la Bastille, through rue St. Antoine and rue Rivoli, to the "Grand Hotel de l' Europe." This hotel, like Paris itself, has no rival or equal in all this hemisphere. And here I think 'tis useless to continue my narrative of a story of three weeks. The Boulevards, the Tuilleries, the Palais Royal, the Gallery of the Louvre, the

Champs Elysees, Bois de Boulogne, Hotel des Invalides, Hotel de Cluny, Hotel de la Ville, the thousand spots of interest here one must visit to realize. My friend and traveling companion, Mr. Ward, arrived here on Sunday last from Rome, (this being the 20th of March), and we have secured, through Mr. Russell Sturgis, passage per Cunard steamer, "Persia," for America, to sail on the 30th inst. I can discern in the political horizon of France that the emperor and the *armée* hold a despotic sway, however much H. I. M. may make it palatable to the people in other respects. No barriers can now be raised in Paris. The new Boulevard runs from the Place Bastile to the Bois de Boulogne, and also longitudinally through Paris. The zouaves are unpopular with the people, and a wide difference exists between the ruler and the governed. By a French paper yesterday, I noticed that 455 soldiers had been pardoned, who were under orders for punishment for offences, besides some 150 more were also to be released ; this by order of the emperor, at the suggestion of the Ministre d' Etat. When were several hundred citizens pardoned of their offences? And does not this take the form of catering to the wishes of this powerful body—the army of France?

Sunday, 23d March. After a stay of over two weeks here in Paris, I take my leave, in company with Mr. Ward and Lieut. Col. Ripley, U. S. A., by rail for Boulogne, Folkstone and London. We reached Boulogne at 5 P.M., where after passing two hours for the steamer to secure a suitable tide, we crossed the Channel and took rail at Folkstone ; reaching London at 11 P.M. The scenery through France, between Paris and Boulogne, does not compare with that between London

and Liverpool, presenting neither high cultivation nor
a thickly-settled country. March 29th. To-day at
10 A.M., we three left London by rail for Liverpool.
A beautiful ride of seven hours it is too ; the scenery
more than counteracts for hours in the cars. Went
to the Tower, Westminster Abbey, through Thames
Tunnel, to the new Houses of Parliament, drove
through Hyde Park and visited the surroundings of
Buckingham Palace, St. James Park, etc., etc. We
lived at Fenton's Hotel, in St. James' Street, had our
meals in our dining-room attached to our parlor and
chambers ; the best living in a hotel I have ever experienced. The sight of St. Paul's Cathedral did not
impress me as did other cathedrals upon the continent,
though larger. Beneath this church one is shown the
tombs of Wellington and Nelson among others. But
the tombs of the illustrious dead at Westminster, render that church or abbey a spot of wonderful interest.
Kings, queens, those who were great as statesmen,
soldiers, poets, naval and remarkable men in England's
history, lie close together throughout the extent of this
vast pile. At 5 P.M. we reached Liverpool, and after
staying all night at the Adelphi Hotel, we left the pier
at 10 A.M., 30th March, for the Cunard steamer "Persia," lying in the river. In a quarter of an hour we
were on board. Mr. Ward and myself occupying a
state-room together and Col. Ripley next to us. At
11 A.M. we sailed with 110 passengers for New York,
via, Cork or Queenstown. At 9 A. M., Sunday, 31st.
March, we arrived at Queenstown and sailed same
evening at four. April 9th, 1861, New York Hotel,
New York City. We arrived here this morning, in
eight days and sixteen hours from Cork, and nine days

twenty hours from Liverpool ; one of the best if not *the* best passage ever made across the Atlantic. We had easterly winds daily, often strong, making fourteen to sixteen knots an hour. Saw no ice, though we experienced snow storms and very cold, foggy, rough weather on the banks. Saw no ship near enough to speak, except the Cunard steamer "Europa," the second day we were out, and the New York packet-ship, "Chancellor," yesterday, off George's Shoal. We had pleasant passengers, though with but one or two exceptions they were not remarkably desirable as future acquaintances. A German lady and her brother I selected as the most attractive—residents of Baltimore. Captain Judkins, who commands the "Persia," is the Nestor of the line, and will soon leave her to take the new steamer "Scotia." His excellent seamanship was attested to by Mr. Ward in a brief dinner speech at table, upon our last day at sea. And now we find ourselves removed from the noble ship which has borne us over the Atlantic, into a little steam-tug alongside, and transported with our baggage over to Jersey City, where in a spacious shed or building, our luggage goes through the custom-house ordeal; which in my case was not very rigid. I had the pleasure of being the direct means of my German lady friend and brother having their trunks quietly passed without examination, which delighted them. And now here we all separate, who for days have been so pleasantly brought together on board ship. I took a vehicle for the New York Hotel, as my traveling companion selected it; though I usually live at the Astor when in New York. And here, therefore, must end my narrative.

After having journeyed through the East and over Europe, through countries with no governments, and with governments the most absolute, where we have in our youth been taught to look with reason for events the most sanguinary and destructive to human interests; contrasting then the beautiful and harmonious working of our own beloved republic with the probable future before those states across the water; I find that the scale has turned, and that while these European and eastern nations are at peace, our own land is rent asunder by groundless evils, by disloyalty of its people, by public and private cupidity, and our own entire territory is likely to become one vast theatre of combat, such as the history of France has often recorded upon its pages—though here upon a vaster scale. I have neither the room, the time or the disposition to consider farther the evils which cloud the horizon of the future of this country; but I trust that they may be averted by a kind Providence, and that our nation may experience its mercy rather than the visitation of its displeasure. Wishing every one who journeys from China, overland, as pleasant a trip as I have had myself, I conclude.

H. P. B.

www.ingramcontent.com/pod-product-compliance
Lightning Source LLC
Chambersburg PA
CBHW032033090426
42733CB00031B/819